CENGAGE Learning

Novels for Students, Volume 8

Staff

Series Editor: Deborah A. Stanley.

Contributing Editors: Peg Bessette, Sara L. Constantakis, Catherine L. Goldstein, Dwayne D. Hayes, Motoko Fujishiro Huthwaite, Arlene M. Johnson, Angela Yvonne Jones, James E. Person, Jr., Polly Rapp, Erin White.

Editorial Technical Specialist: Tim White.

Managing Editor: Joyce Nakamura.

Research: Victoria B. Cariappa, *Research Team Manager*. Andy Malonis, *Research Specialist*. Tamara C. Nott, Tracie A. Richardson, and Cheryl L. Warnock, *Research Associates*. Jeffrey Daniels, *Research Assistant*.

Permissions: Susan M. Trosky, *Permissions Manager*. Maria L. Franklin, *Permissions Specialist*. Sarah Tomacek, *Permissions Associate*.

Production: Mary Beth Trimper, *Production Director*. Evi Seoud, *Assistant Production Manager*. Cindy Range, *Production Assistant*.

Graphic Services: Randy Bassett, *Image Database Supervisor*. Robert Duncan and Michael Logusz, *Imaging Specialists*. Pamela A. Reed, *Photography Coordinator*. Gary Leach, *Macintosh Artist*.

Product Design: Cynthia Baldwin, *Product Design Manager*. Cover Design: Michelle DiMercurio, *Art Director*. Page Design: Pamela A. E. Galbreath, *Senior Art Director*.

Ten Little Indians

Agatha Christie 1939

Introduction

In 1939 mystery lovers eagerly awaited the publication of Agatha Christie's new novel, *Ten Little Indians*. They were not disappointed. The novel soon became a best-seller, gaining critical success along with its popularity. First published in England as *Ten Little Niggers*, the book was renamed *And Then There Were None*, from the closing line of the nursery rhyme, for publication in the United States. The original title was deemed too offensive for the American public. Later, the title would be changed to *Ten Little Indians*.

The novel focuses on a group of people invited

by a mysterious Mr. Owen to enjoy a holiday on Indian Island. After the guests start turning up dead, the mystery deepens. Tension mounts as the remaining guests attempt to discover the murderer's identity before they are all killed. After Christie adapted the novel for the stage, it enjoyed successful runs in both England and America and was twice adapted for film. It has also been translated into several different languages. Critics praise the novel's intricate plotting and innovative technique, noting that in it, Christie adds new twists to the mystery genre. Most scholars, along with her devoted fans, consider *Ten Little Indians* to be one of the best mystery novels ever written.

Agatha Christie sets *Ten Little Indians* on an island that lies off the coast of Devon, England, where she grew up. She was born on September 15, 1890, in Torquay, a resort town on the Devon coast. Her parents, American Frederick Miller and Clarissa Boehmer Miller, born in Ireland, raised her and her two siblings in an upper-middle-class atmosphere. She grew up among a mix of landed gentry, retired military officers who had served in remote British colonies, and farmers. Robin Winks in *British Writers* notes that Christie "drew upon the reality, and even more the memories and myths, of her childhood for many of her settings and characters." This appears true, also, in her creation of the mix of characters in *Ten Little Indians*.

In 1914, she married Colonel Archibald Christie, a member of the Flying Corps, and soon after worked as a nurse during World War I. Fourteen years later the marriage ended in divorce. While traveling in the Middle East, Christie met and later married archaeologist Max Mallowan, whom she accompanied on many archaeological digs. On a dare from her sister, she wrote her first detective novel, *The Mysterious Affair at Styles*, published in 1920. That and the four other novels that followed were well received, but it took the publication of her next novel, *The Murder of Roger Ackroyd*, in 1926 to gain her the reputation of one of the world's most popular writers. Known as the "Grand Dame" of mysteries, or as she preferred, the "Duchess of Death," Christie was also a most prolific writer. Her works include almost one hundred mystery novels and short-story collections, six romantic novels under the pen name Mary Westmacott, twenty-one plays, and a two-volume autobiography. Many of her works have been translated into more than one hundred languages.

Christie earned several awards and honors during her career, including the Mystery Writers of America Grand Master Award and the honor of D.B.E. (Dame Commander, Order of the British Empire), conferred upon her by Queen Elizabeth. When she died on January 12, 1976, at her home in Wallingford, Oxfordshire, London theatres dimmed their lights, offering a fitting tribute to this internationally acclaimed author.

Part I

In *Ten Little Indians* Christie creates a masterpiece of mystery and murder. After ten strangers gather together on an isolated island off the coast of Devon, England, one by one, they each are discovered murdered. As those remaining frantically search for the murderer, their own guilty pasts return to haunt them.

Mr. Justice Wargrave, lately retired from the bench, travels by train to Devon where he will be taken by boat to Indian Island. Seven others are also on their way there, most invited by a Mr. or Mrs. Owen. Vera Claythorne, a young, attractive teacher was hired through a letter from Una Nancy Owen for a short stint as a secretary. Captain Philip Lombard is not sure why he has been assigned to the island, other than to hold himself "at the disposal of a client." Miss Emily Brent, an elderly woman, has been invited by letter by someone she met years ago at a guesthouse. General Macarthur, retired from service, was invited by "a man named Owen" to "chat about old times" and Dr. Armstrong was asked by letter to treat Mrs. Owen's medical condition. Dashing young Tony Marston also received a letter from the Owens inviting him to the island. None of them, however, are very clear about who the Owens are. While Mr. Blore travels by train to the island, he writes down the names of the seven people we have just met along with two servants, Mr. and Mrs. Rogers, and decides to pretend to be a Mr. Davis. As Fred Narracott, a local sailor, takes them all to Indian Island by boat, Vera notes "there was something sinister" about it and "shivered faintly."

After they arrive at the island, Mr. Rogers, the butler, tells them that Mr. Owen has been "unfortunately delayed" and will not appear until the next day. Mrs. Rogers, the cook, shows them to their rooms and they later reunite for dinner where they discover ten little china Indians on a table. They also note that the "Ten Little Indians" nursery rhyme is framed in each of their rooms. After dinner an "inhuman" voice penetrates the comfortable silence surrounding the group, charging that each of them has been responsible for a death and concluding with, "Prisoners at the bar, have you anything to say in your defense?"

When asked, Rogers tells the rest that he put on the record, *Swan Song*, as per instructions written in a letter from Mr. Owen. Justice Wargrave immediately takes charge and converts the room into "an impromptu court of law." Rogers explains that he never met Owen and that all orders were sent by letter. The guests decide to pool their information about how they were invited, but Lombard doesn't reveal why he is there. When pressed, Blore, an ex-policeman who now runs a detective agency, admits he was hired by Owen to watch his wife's jewels. Wargrave concludes that the person who invited them is unknown to them and "no doubt ... is a madman—probably a dangerous homicidal lunatic."

The guests then claim to be innocent of the charges leveled against them. Wargrave insists his conscience is perfectly clear about passing sentence on Edward Seton "a rightly convicted murderer." Armstrong, however, remembers hearing comments about how the judge was against Seton and so turned the jury around to a guilty verdict. Vera explains that she was hired as nursery governess to Cyril Hamilton who one day swam out too far and drowned before she could reach him. The General declares there to be no truth to the accusation that he murdered Arthur Richmond, one of his officers. He explains that he sent Richmond on a reconnaissance where he was killed "in the natural course of events in war time."

Lombard, on the other hand, admits the story about him is true. While in the bush, he left a group of natives behind to die as a "matter of self-preservation." He justifies his actions by arguing that "natives don't mind dying…. They don't feel about it as Europeans do." Marston decides that John and Lucy Combes "must have been a couple of kids I ran over near Cambridge" and insists the incident was "pure accident." Rogers explains that he and his wife called the doctor for Miss Brady, whom they cared for, but the doctor didn't come in time. When pressed, he admits that after she died, they received an inheritance from her. Blore confesses that he got a promotion from providing evidence to convict James Landor, who later died in jail, but asserts that he "was only doing [his] duty." Dr. Armstrong tells the others that he can't remember Louisa Clees, but thinks about the night he got drunk and operated on her, acknowledging to himself, "I killed her." Emily insists, "I have nothing with which to reproach myself."

Part II

After they all agree to leave in the morning when Narracott comes in the boat with supplies, Marston gulps down his drink, chokes, and falls down dead. The others decide he must have committed suicide by putting something into his drink. After they go to bed, some think about the accusations against them. Wargrave insists Seton was guilty, but Macarthur admits that he deliberately sent Richmond to his death after discovering his affair with his wife. In the morning they discover Rogers's wife dead and only eight Indian figures left on the table. They note that the deaths of Marston and Mrs. Rogers fit the descriptions in the nursery rhyme. When the boat doesn't come, they realize they are trapped on the island. Emily later admits to Vera that when Beatrice Taylor, her servant, got pregnant, Emily fired her and she committed suicide. Emily, though, reiterates her own innocence. Lombard, Blore, and Armstrong search the island and the house for Mr. Owen but find nothing. When they conclude that there is no one else on the island except the eight of them, they become terrified and start to suspect each other.

In the afternoon the General is found dead, hit on the back of the head. That evening as a storm rages outside, they eye each other suspiciously. The next morning they find Rogers murdered while chopping wood and note that after each murder, an Indian figure disappears. Later, Blore admits to Lombard that Landor was innocent and that he had been coerced into framing him. After breakfast they find Emily dead from an injection and that evening discover the judge shot through the head. The next day Lombard pressures Vera into admitting she engineered Cyril's death so that Hugo, her lover, could inherit a great deal of money and be free to marry her. Later when they discover Blore and Armstrong have also been murdered, they turn on each other and Vera shoots him. Exhausted Vera goes to her room and finds a rope fashioned into a noose hanging from a hook in the ceiling. She thinks, "that's what Hugo wanted," and hangs herself.

Part III

The narrative then shifts to a conversation between Sir Thomas Legge, Assistant Commissioner at Scotland Yard, and Inspector Maine about what happened on the island. Inspector Maine recounts how each died and tells the Commissioner that Isaac Morris, an "unsavory" man mixed up in drug dealing, made all the arrangements at the island and covered his employer's tracks. Morris was later found dead of an overdose of sleeping medication. Maine reviews the accusations from the record and can clear only Wargrave absolutely, noting Seton was "unmistakably guilty." However, Maine has not been able to uncover the murderer's identity.

The novel ends with a transcript of a manuscript found stuffed in a bottle by a fishing trawler and sent to Scotland Yard. The manuscript, a written confession by Wargrave, explains how his contradictory desires for justice and murder prompted him to plan something "stupendous ... something theatrical." Through conversations with people he met, he learned of the guilty past of each of the nine. After he discovered himself to be terminally ill, he bought Indian Island and lured the others there and one by one, murdered them. With Armstrong's help, he faked his death so the mystery would not be discovered. Morris, whom he poisoned before he came to the island, was his tenth victim. After arranging for the deaths of the others, Wargrave shot himself in the same manner in which he appeared to be shot earlier. His desire to show off his ingenious scheme prompted him to place his confession in the bottle.

Dr. Edward Armstrong

Dr. Armstrong is coming to Indian Island to examine and treat Mrs. Owen after receiving a letter from her husband. He takes pleasure in a reputation as "a good man at his job" and so has enjoyed a great deal of success. However, "he was very tired.... Success had its penalties." As he travels to Devon, he alludes to a past incident that occurred fifteen years ago that "had been a near thing." During that period, he notes that he had been "going to pieces," and the shock of the traumatic event prompted him to give up drinking. Later his thoughts about the incident reveal that his drunken performance in the operating room killed Louisa Clees. While on the island, Armstrong is a bundle of nerves. His gullibility leads him to help Wargrave carry out his plans, which include murdering Armstrong.

William Blore

William Blore pretends to be Mr. Davis, a "man of means from South Africa," sure that "he could enter into any society unchallenged." His true identity as a detective hired to watch Mrs. Owen's jewels is quickly and easily exposed soon after he arrives at Indian Island. The narrator describes him as "an earnest man" and notes that "a light touch was incomprehensible to him." Lombard observes his lack of imagination. After discovering that Blore committed perjury during the bank robbery trial that resulted in the conviction of an innocent man, Inspector Maine declares him to be "a bad hat."

Miss Emily Brent

Miss Emily Brent, a "hard and self-righteous" sixty-five-year-old woman, received a letter signed "UN" from someone claiming to have met her years ago at a guesthouse. Her repressed nature becomes immediately apparent as she sits "upright" in the train, because she "did not approve of lounging." She agrees with her father, "a Colonel of the old school," who thought "the present generation was shamelessly lax—in their carriage, and in every other way." She sits in the compartment, "enveloped in an aura of righteousness and unyielding principles." Since her income has been lately reduced, she looks forward to a free holiday at Indian Island. When she hears the voice on the record accuse her of murder, she becomes "encased in her own armour of virtue," and insists "I had nothing with which to reproach myself." When Vera asks her whether she has been affected by the murders that have been taking place on the island, Emily responds, "I was brought up to keep my head and never to make a fuss." Vera concludes that this confession proves that Emily must have been repressed in her childhood and so explains her inability to respond normally to what has happened on the island. Emily eventually admits to Vera that when Beatrice Taylor, her servant, got pregnant, Emily fired her and she committed suicide. Emily, though, reiterates her own innocence.

Vera Claythorne

Vera Claythorne is an attractive young woman who comes to Indian Island expecting employment as a secretary after receiving a letter from Una Nancy Owen. Lombard describes her as "a cool customer ... one who could hold her own—in love or war," an ironic foreshadowing of her composure as she fatally shoots him. She shows an ambitious nature when she hopes that this temporary job will lead to a more desirable permanent position and so allow her to leave the "third-class school" where she has been teaching.

Throughout the novel, she appears troubled about an incident in her past, which we later learn is the drowning of Cyril Hamilton, a young boy in her care. Her first thoughts reveal her love for and sorrow over her dissolved relationship with Hugo Hamilton, the boy's uncle. She also appears to feel guilt over the boy's death. Soon though we learn of her cruel and selfish nature when she finally acknowledges her part in Cyril's death. She admits that she encouraged the "whiny spoilt little brat" to swim out too far into the water, knowing he would not be able to make it back to shore. Trying to justify her actions, she notes, "if it weren't for him, Hugo would be rich" and able to marry her.

Wargrave finds her to be an "interesting

psychological experiment" after all the other guests have been murdered. He wondered, "would the consciousness of her own guilt, the state of nervous tension consequent on having just shot a man, be sufficient, together with the hypnotic suggestion of the surroundings, to cause her to take her own life." Vera proves Wargrave's hypothesis when she hangs herself. He deems her crime to be the most heinous, because he plots her demise only after she experiences the murders of all the others.

Mr. Davis

See William Blore

Sir Thomas Legge

Sir Thomas Legge, Assistant Commissioner at Scotland Yard tries to solve the mystery of what happened on Indian Island with Inspector Maine, who has been investigating the case. Legge becomes infuriated when he cannot.

Captain Philip Lombard

Captain Philip Lombard sits opposite Vera on the train to Indian Island. He is not sure why he has been assigned to the island, other than the fact that he is "at the disposal of a client." Issac Morris, the agent who hired him, considers him to be "a good man in a tight place." Lombard admits that in his past actions, "legality had not always been a sine qua non.... There wasn't much he'd draw the line at." He had previously been mixed up in shady business abroad which gained him "a reputation for daring and for not being overscrupulous" about murder. He exhibits this latter quality when he admits to the others that he did cause the death of twenty-one East African men. In an attempt to justify his actions, he explains that while in the bush, he left the natives behind to die as a "matter of self-preservation." He insists, "natives don't mind dying.... They don't feel about it as Europeans do." Due to the callous nature of his crime, Wargrave allows him to suffer longer than the others before he is murdered.

General Gordon Macarthur

General Macarthur has received a letter from a man named Owen inviting him to Indian Island to "chat about old times." Macarthur's guilt about his past becomes evident in his paranoid notion that people have been avoiding him lately because of "that damned rumour" about an incident that occurred thirty years ago. He thinks that people suspect that he really did send Arthur Richmond to his death. As a result, he has slowly withdrawn from others and into himself. At the island he thinks about Richmond's affair with his wife and his subsequent decision to send him on a deadly reconnaissance. His guilt over his actions prompts his decision that he's "come to the end of things" and that he doesn't want to leave the island. At one point, the other guests find a dazed Macarthur looking out to sea exclaiming, "there is so little time.... I really must insist that no one disturbs me." He later explains to Vera, "none of us are going to leave the island" and expresses his relief that he won't have to "carry the burden any longer."

Inspector Maine

Inspector Maine reports to Sir Thomas Legge, Assistant Commissioner at Scotland Yard. He has investigated the murders at Indian Island and has discovered background information on some of the guests. However, he has not been able to solve the case.

Media Adaptations

- Christie adapted *Ten Little Indians* for the stage. It first played with the novel's original title, *Ten Little Niggers*, in London, opening October 17, 1943; it was produced under the title *Ten Little Indians* on Broadway and opened at the Broadhurst Theatre on June 27, 1944.

- The novel was made into three film versions, all titled *Ten Little Indians*. The first (1966) was directed by George Pollock and starred Hugh O'Brian and Shirley Eaton. The second (1974) was directed by Peter Collinson and starred Oliver Reed and Richard Attenborough. The third (1989) was directed by Alan Birkinshaw, starring Donald Pleasence and Brenda Vaccaro.

Anthony Marston

Anthony Marston has been invited through letter by a friend to visit the Owens on Indian Island. Marston is handsome, young, and "a creature of sensation—and of action." His reckless actions, specifically his speeding, cause the death of two young people, John and Lucy Combes. His "complete callousness and his inability to feel any responsibility for the lives he had taken," prompt Wargrave to dispose of him first. Wargrave knows that Marston's amoral nature would prevent him from experiencing any guilt over his past and thus from feeling an increasing sense of unease as the murder plot unfolds. Wargrave murders Marston because his recklessness proves him to be "a danger to the community."

Isaac Morris

Isaac Morris, an "unsavory" man mixed up in drug deals, made all the arrangements at the island. He put the Indian Island house sale through a third party so the buyer would not be discovered and then carefully covered the buyer's tracks. Wargrave kills him with an overdose of drugs before he leaves for the island.

Fred Narracott

Fred Narracott, a local sailor, takes the others by boat to the island. He is "a man of the sea, [with] a weather-beaten face and dark eyes with a slightly evasive expression." Like the other residents of Sticklehaven, he feels uneasy about what is happening on the island, noting "the whole thing was queer—very queer."

Mrs. Ethel Rogers

Mrs. Rogers, wife of the butler Mr. Rogers, serves as cook and maid for the guests at Indian Island. The guests note that she is "a white bloodless ghost of a woman" and that her "flat-monotonous voice" and "queer light shifty eyes" make her look like a woman "who walked in mortal fear." Wargrave decides to murder her early on, since he feels her husband coerced her into neglecting the health of her previous employer, Jennifer Brady.

Mr. Thomas Rogers

Mr. Rogers was hired as a butler to serve the guests at Indian Island. Never having met his employer, he obeys all orders sent to him by letter, including the playing of the record that accuses all the guests, including himself and his wife, of murder. Even after he discovers his wife murdered, he remains "the good servant," carrying on "with an impassive countenance." We later discover that he and his wife had intentionally waited too long to call the doctor when their elderly employer, Jennifer Brady, fell ill. After her death, the couple gained a substantial inheritance.

Mr. Justice Lawrence Wargrave

Mr. Justice Wargrave, retired from the law, is a distinguished looking gentleman on his way to Indian Island after being invited there by letter from his friend, Constance Culmington. Upon closer inspection, however, the guests notice that his "pale shrewd little eyes" and "hunched up attitude" suggest a "decidedly reptilian" demeanor. He has been reputed to have "great powers with a jury," but some call him "a hanging judge." When he takes out his false teeth, his "shrunken lips" compress and turn his mouth "cruel" and "predatory." At the end of the novel, Wargrave is found innocent of the charge that he wrongfully helped convict Edward

Seton but guilty of murdering all the guests at Indian Island.

In the document discovered in a bottle and sent to Scotland Yard, he confesses to his crimes and reveals relevant character details: "From my earliest youth I realized that my nature was a mass of contradictions" including an "incurably romantic imagination," a "sadistic delight in seeing or causing death" and a "strong sense of justice." He explains that these contradictions prompted him to go into law, since "the legal profession satisfied nearly all [his] instincts." Wargrave further admits, "to see a wretched criminal squirming in the dock, suffering the tortures of the damned, as his doom came slowly and slowly nearer, was to me, an exquisite pleasure." And so, he lured ten guilty people to Indian Island and murdered them theatrically and slowly, one at a time.

Appearances and Reality

The focus on appearance versus reality appears throughout the novel in the form of the underlying theme of deception. All the characters deceive others and sometimes themselves about their true natures. All profess to be good, but in reality are filled with evil in the form of moral corruption caused by intolerance, jealousy, greed, and desire. The action begins under a cloud of deception when Judge Wargrave, under the guise of the mysterious Mr. Owen, lures the group to Indian Island. The deception continues after the voice on the recording accuses each of a crime and they all deny any responsibility. Wargrave's confession reveals the final deception when he exposes his faked murder and his own true nature.

Fear of Death

As soon as bodies start appearing on the island, the remaining guests are enveloped by the fear of death. Their instincts for survival cause them to suspect each other. As a result their primitive instincts emerge: Wargrave's mouth turns "cruel and predatory," Lombard's smile resembles that of a wolf, and Blore appears "coarser and clumsier" with "a look of mingled ferocity and stupidity about him."

Guilt and Innocence

The novel ties the question of the characters' guilt or innocence to the theme of appearance versus reality. At the beginning of their stay on the island, all the guests claim to be innocent. Some insist their crimes were committed by accident. Tony Marston explains that the accident that caused the deaths of John and Lucy Combes was "beastly bad luck." Louisa Clees' death, caused by Dr. Armstrong's drunken state in the operating room, was also accidental. The two, however, respond differently to these accidents. Marston will claim no responsibility. His amoral nature compounds his guilt. Armstrong, on the other hand, recognizes his responsibility for his patient's death, but cannot admit it publicly. Lombard's claims of innocence stem from the same kind of amoral nature coupled with his racism. He dismisses his "crime" arguing that his own survival should take precedence over that of the natives. Christie complicates the question of guilt and innocence when the focus turns to Wargrave. Is the judge guilty of the murder of ten people or is he fulfilling his duty as judge? His description of his motives in his confession point to his guilt.

Justice and Injustice

Justice is served when the guilty are punished. Injustice occurs when the innocent are punished. Wargrave justifies his crimes by claiming that the ten deserved to die because they victimized innocent people. He prompts us then to consider his victims not truly victims. Acting as judge, jury, and executioner, his punishment, he insists, was just.

Sanity and Insanity

Four people on the island experience varying degrees of insanity, due for the most part to feelings of overwhelming guilt. Dr. Armstrong's guilt clouds his judgment when Wargrave asks him for help in staging his own murder. Afterwards, his nervous state propels him close to the point of collapse. Macarthur's guilt preys on him before he arrives on the island, taking the form of paranoia. He suspects people are whispering about his crime behind his back and so withdraws from society. While on the island, he appears to fall into a trance, muttering to the others that he wants to be left alone. Immediately before Wargrave kills him, he admits that he does not want to ever leave the island. He appears to welcome his impending death as he looks forward to not having to "carry the burden any longer." Throughout the novel, the judge appears to feel the burden of guilt less than anyone does. However, in his confession he reveals himself to be the very "homicidal maniac" he told the others to be on guard against.

Topics for Further Study

- Conduct a mock trial for Justice Wargrave to determine whether or not he should be convicted of first-degree murder. If he is convicted, determine his sentence.

- Research English culture and determine whether or not the characters would behave any differently if they were American instead of British.

- Read another mystery story and compare the two works, focusing on how the mystery in each is constructed.

- Investigate psychologists' conclusions on the nature of the criminal mind and compare those findings to the characterization of

Justice Wargrave.

Style

Structure

The novel is structured as a mystery, although Christie adds her own innovations. Stories of good versus evil have been told since the beginning of time, but the mystery story emerged in the second half of the nineteenth century with the works of Edgar Allan Poe and Arthur Conan Doyle. The mystery structure includes motives and alibis, detection, clues, and red herrings (diversions from the real culprit). Characters become suspects before the true one is unmasked. The hero discovers the villain only at the climax of the story, and then, in the denouement, explains how the crime was committed. Christie carries on several of the traditions of the mystery but adds some new twists. The characters in *Ten little Indians* present motives for past crimes and alibis for the murders on the island. Judge Wargrave, who at the end of the novel, identifies the murderer and puts all the pieces of the puzzle back together, engineers detection, clues, and a red herring. Christie's twist on the traditional mystery structure is that all of the characters are discovered to be villains; none are innocent. The final irony and delightful innovative turn is that the hidden villain in the novel, Judge Wargrave, also becomes the "hero," in the modern sense of the term.

Symbol

Christie uses the setting symbolically in the novel. The house becomes a symbol of the characters' fate. As the others search for "Mr. Owen," the narrator notes, "If this had been an old house, with creaking wood, and dark shadows, and heavily paneled walls, there might have been an eerie feeling. But this house was the essence of modernity. There were no dark corners—no possible sliding panels—it was flooded with electric light—everything was new and bright and shining. There was nothing hidden in this house, nothing concealed. It had no atmosphere about it. Somehow, that was the most frightening thing of all." As the narrator notes, nothing can be hidden in this house, especially the guilt of all the guests who inhabit it. The manner of death Wargrave chooses for himself is also symbolic, and he uses it as a clue to the real identity of the murderer on the island. He arranges to shoot himself in his forehead, the first time as a trick and the second time for real. In his confession, he notes that the mark in his head is symbolic of the "brand of Cain."

Foreshadowing

This technique occurs when an old man sitting across from Blore on the train warns, "there's a squall ahead … Watch and pray…. The day of judgment is at hand." A squall will hit the island, literally and figuratively, and judgment will be pronounced and acted upon.

World War II

The world experienced a decade of aggression in the 1930s that would culminate in World War II. This second world war resulted from the rise of totalitarian regimes in Germany, Italy, and Japan. These militaristic regimes gained control as a result of the great depression experienced by most of the world in the early 1930s and from the condi-tions created by the peace settlements following World War I. The dictatorships established in each country encouraged expansion into neighboring countries. In Germany Hitler strengthened the army during the 1930s. In 1936 Benito Mussolini's Italian troops took Ethiopia. From 1936 to 1939 Spain was engaged in civil war involving Francisco Franco's fascist army, aided by Germany and Italy. In March 1938 Germany annexed Austria and in March 1939 occupied Czechoslovakia. Italy took Albania in April 1939. One week after Nazi Germany and the U.S.S.R. signed a Treaty of Nonag-gression, on September 1, 1939, Germany invaded Poland and World War II began. On September 3, 1939, Britain and France declared war on Germany after a U-boat sank the British ship *Athenia* off the coast of Ireland. Another British ship, *Courageous*, was sunk on September 19. All the members of the British Commonwealth, except Ireland, soon joined Britain and France in their declaration of war.

Ten Little Indians was published in 1939, the year World War II began. While the novel is set in an indeterminate time period, Christie's focus on the darker side of human nature coincides with the displays of aggression evident in the 1930s. Her use of English characters and setting does not seem to contain much cultural significance. The novel does not portray genteel English characters who pride themselves on their sportsmanlike behavior.

Critical Overview

Ten Little Indians has been a popular and critical success since its publication in 1939. This best-selling novel appeared during what critics determine to be Christie's most productive period, from 1926 to the early 1950s. Many consider *Ten Little Indians* to be her best work.

Scholars note that Christie owes a debt to earlier crime writers such as Anna Katharine Green and Arthur Conan Doyle, yet most agree that she has had a tremendous influence on the crime novel genre. In *British Writers* Robin Winks observes her link to past works and her influence on future writers when he declares the novel to be "markedly tense, as close to a gothic thriller and modern suspense novel as the author would come." He insists that "Christie was original because of the way in which she developed plot, unraveled motive, and put utterly fresh twists on timeworn devices." He applauds her "quite remarkable ability to build motive, to misdirect the reader and to weave complex plots that turned and turned again."

Compare & Contrast

- **1930s:** The economy collapses and causes a decade of poverty and hunger for millions of people.
  Today: The economy is booming,

but many fear the year 2000 could cause another period of economic crisis.

- **1930s:** World War II begins in 1939. The United States plans to remain neutral in the war, until its ships are attacked at Pearl Harbor in 1941.
  Today: The United States helps control the 1999 crisis in Kosovo through air strikes and is able to keep from deploying ground troops.

- **1930s:** Adolf Hitler becomes chancellor of Germany in 1933. His dictatorship promises order for his country, but instead, results in fear, suffering, war, and death for many of its citizens, especially the Jewish population.
  Today: Many survivors of Hitler's rule and their families who have reestablished their lives—many in the United States—are still trying to heal the pain stemming from Hitler's murderous tactics.

Commenting on her style, Winks suggests that Christie was "at her best a writer of clear and engaging prose, a gentle (and at times sly) social critic, and a master of that element so essential to storytelling—plot." In his article on *Ten Little Indians* and *Murder on the Orient Express* for the

Spectator, Anthony Lejeune writes that these works are "famous because each of them turns on a piece of misdirection and a solution which, in their day, were startlingly innovatory." Ralph Partridge's review in *New Statesman* asserts, "Apart from one little dubious proceeding there is no cheating; the reader is just bamboozled in a straightforward way from first to last. To show her utter superiority over our deductive faculty, from time to time Mrs. Christie even allows us to know what every character present is thinking and still we can't guess!" Julian Symons praises her construction of puzzles in the novel and in her other works in his *Mortal Consequences: A History—From the Detective Story to the Crime Novel:* "Agatha Christie's claim to supremacy among the classical detective story writers of her time rests on her originality in contructing puzzles. This was her supreme skill.... If her work survives it will be because she was the supreme mistress of a magical skill that is a permanent, although often secret, concern of humanity: the construction and the solution of puzzles."

Some, however, have found fault with Christie's style. A few scholars criticize the genre itself, finding mysteries in general to pander to popular, uneducated tastes. Others discover limitations in what they consider to be the formulaic style of Christie's writing. They complain that her characters are stereotypical, and that the plots are too predictable and lack depth. Some note examples of racism, classicism, and sexism in her work. Marty S. Knepper, in "Agatha Christie—Feminist," argues that her novels, including *Ten Little Indians*, "present women in totally stereotypical ways: as empty-headed ingenues, for example, or as gossipy old ladies."

Despite the reservations of some critics, Agatha Christie remains today one of the world's most popular and highly acclaimed authors, a position noted by Max Lowenthal in his summary of her work in the *New York Times*, written after her death in 1976. He writes, "Dame Agatha's forte was supremely adroit plotting and sharp, believable characterization.... Her style and rhetoric were not remarkable; her writing was almost invariably sound and workmanlike, without pretense of flourish. Her characters were likely to be of the middle-middle class or upper-middle class, and there were certain archetypes, such as the crass American or the stuffy retired army officer now in his anecdotage. However familiar all this might be, the reader would turn the pages mesmerized as unexpected twist piled on unexpected twist until, in the end, he was taken by surprise. There was simply no outguessing ... Agatha Christie."

What Do I Read Next?

- In *Murder on the Orient Express* (1934) Agatha Christie writes a variation on *Ten Little Indians*, gathering together a diverse set of characters and focusing on the murder of one of them. This time, though, Hercule Poirot, a Belgian detective, solves the crime.

- Dorothy L. Sayers's *Strong Poison* (1930) centers on Lord Peter Wimsey's determination to find out who poisoned novelist Harriet Vane's fiancé.

- *The Adventures of Sherlock Holmes*, a collection of short stories published in 1892, introduces Sir Arthur Conan Doyle's famous detective and his sidekick, Dr.

Watson, in four classic mysteries.

- In P. D. James's *Innocent Blood* (1980) Philippa Palfrey meets her biological mother and discovers the shocking mystery that surrounds her.

Sources

Stewart H. Benedict, "Agatha Christie and Murder Most Unsportsmanlike," in *Claremont Quarterly*, Vol. 9, No. 2, Winter, 1962, pp. 37-42.

David Grossvogel, *Death Deferred: The Long Life, Splendid Afterlife, and Mysterious Workings of Agatha Christie*, Johns Hopkins University Press, 1979.

Marty S. Knepper, "Agatha Christie-Feminist," in *The Armchair Detective*, Vol. 16, No. 4, Winter, 1983, pp. 398-406.

Anthony Lejeune, review in *Spectator*, September 19, 1970.

Max Lowenthal, obituary in *New York Times*, January 13, 1976, p. 1.

Ralph Partridge, review in *New Statesman*, November 18, 1939.

Julian Symons, *Mortal Consequences: A History-From the Detective Story to the Crime Novel*, Harper, 1972.

Robin W. Winks, *British Writers, Supplement 2*, Scribner's, 1992, pp. 123-37.

For Further Study

Agatha Christie: First Lady of Crime, edited by H. R. F. Keating, Holt, Rinehart and Winston, 1977.

> This collection of essays provides biographical details as well as analyses of individual works, including *Ten Little Indians*.

Robert Barnard, *A Talent to Deceive: An Appreciation of Agatha Christie*, Dodd, Mead and Company, 1980.

> Barnard examines Christie's "strategies of deception" in her works, including *Ten Little Indians*.

Nancy Y. Hoffman, "Mistresses of Malfeasance," in *Dimensions of Detective Fiction*, edited by Larry N. Landrum, Pat Browne, and Ray B. Browne, Popular Press, 1976, pp. 97-101.

> This essay compares Christie's style to other women mystery writers.

G. C. Ramsey, *Agatha Christie: Mistress of Mystery*, 1967.

> An early analysis of Christie's work.

CPSIA information can be obtained
at www.ICGtesting.com
Printed in the USA
BVOW09s1742200418
513857BV00001B/11/P